Take a Closer Look at

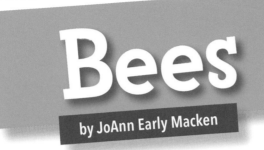

Bees

by JoAnn Early Macken

Content Consultant
Dr. Marla Spivak
Department of Entomology
University of Minnesota

RED CHAIR PRESS™

Please visit our website at www.redchairpress.com for more high-quality products for young readers.

About the Author: JoAnn Early Macken has written more than 130 books for young readers. JoAnn earned her M.F.A. in Writing for Children and Young Adults at Vermont College of Fine Arts. She has taught writing at four Wisconsin colleges, and she speaks about poetry and writing to children and adults at schools, libraries, and conferences.

Publisher's Cataloging-In-Publication Data

Macken, JoAnn Early, 1953-

    Take a closer look at. Bees / by JoAnn Early Macken ; content consultant, Dr. Marla Spivak, Department of Entomology, University of Minnesota. -- [First edition].

    pages : illustrations, maps, charts ; cm

    Summary: Scientists believe that the survival of bees is at risk. What has put bees at risk and should we care? Bees are responsible for pollinating about 70 of the 100 crops that feed 90% of the world. Without bees nearly half the world could starve. In this book, find out how scientists are working on ways to keep bees healthy. STEM career opportunities are featured. Includes a glossary and references for additional reading.

    "Core content library"--Cover.

    Interest age level: 006-010.

    Edition statement supplied by publisher.

    Issued also as an ebook. (ISBN: 978-1-63440-060-2)

    Includes bibliographical references and index.

    ISBN: 978-1-63440-052-7 (library hardcover)

    1. Bees--Juvenile literature. 2. Honeybee--Diseases--Juvenile literature. 3. Food supply--Juvenile literature. 4. Bees. 5. Honeybee--Diseases. 6. Food supply. I. Spivak, Marla. II. Title. III. Title: Take a closer look at bees IV. Title: Bees

QL565.2 .M33 2016

595.79/9   2015937991

Photo credits: Dreamstime: 18; Shutterstock: cover, 3-17, 19-39, 40; Courtesy of The White House: 33 (top)

This series first published by:

Red Chair Press LLC   PO Box 333   South Egremont, MA 01258-0333

Printed in the United States of America

Distributed in the U.S. by Lerner Publisher Services. www.lernerbooks.com

112015 1P LPSS16

Contents

1 Why Are Bees Important to Us?

Picture a bee. What comes to mind? A fuzzy, striped bumblebee? A shiny green sweat bee? A honey bee in a hive? About 20,000 species of bees live around the world. North America is home to 4,000 of them.

Most bees live alone. Some live in small groups. Others form **colonies**. Many bees, such as mining bees, live in holes in the ground. They dig tunnels in sunny spots. Other types take over holes in dead trees bored by beetles or birds. Mason bees build nests from mud. Leaf cutter bees wrap pieces of petals or leaves in their nests. Wool carder bees line their nests with plant fibers.

All bees are insects. They have six legs and three body parts: head, thorax, and abdomen. All bees have two sets of wings. Bees begin their lives as eggs. They change into **larvae** and then **pupae** before they become adults.

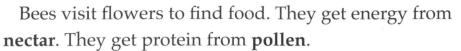

Bees visit flowers to find food. They get energy from **nectar**. They get protein from **pollen**. They also feed pollen to their larvae. While they fly from flower to flower, bees provide a valuable service.

Pollination

How does a plant produce more plants? One way is to make seeds. Plants form seeds in their flowers.

To form seeds, a plant needs pollen. Pollen is made in the **anther**. It germinates, or begins to grow, in the **stigma**. If pollen lands there, fruit and seeds can develop. But something must move the pollen. That something is often a bee.

When a bee feeds in a flower, pollen sticks to its body. It carries the pollen to another flower. Some of it rubs off. The bee **pollinates** the flower by providing the pollen it needs.

Plants flower at different times. That means they don't have to compete for pollinators. And pollinators can find food through the whole growing season.

Bees travel from flower to flower seeking out nectar and pollen.

Some flowers attract bees. Many are bright white, yellow, or blue. Those are the colors a bee can see. A bee also sees something we can't: ultraviolet light. In some flowers, an ultraviolet pattern marks the flower's center. The pattern is called a called a nectar guide. It helps a bee find its way to the nectar. Other flowers attract bees with their scents or the shapes of their petals. Some flowers have landing spots perfect for bees.

Wind and water can also carry pollen. But many flowering plants depend on animal pollinators. That includes most of the world's crop plants. Their fruits and seeds provide as much as one-third of the food we eat. Birds and animals eat fruits and seeds, too.

Almond trees depend entirely on honey bees for pollination.

Some bats and birds also pollinate plants. So do butterflies and moths. Other insects such as flies, beetles, and ants are pollinators. But bees are the most important because bees need pollen for nutrition.

⭐ Many herbs produce flowers that attract bees and butterflies.

Some Food Plants that Bees Pollinate		
Almonds	Cantaloupe	Pears
Apples	Carrots	Plums
Apricots	Cherries	Potatoes
Avocados	Cranberries	Pumpkins
Broadbeans	Cucumber	Rhubarb
Beets	Kale	Squash
Blackberries	Mustard	Strawberries
Blueberries	Melons	Sunflowers
Brussels sprouts	Onions	Sweet potatoes
Cabbage	Peaches	Tomatoes

Honey bees

Honey bees are social insects. In a colony, one queen lays all the eggs. She can lay 1,000 in a day. Female worker bees care for the queen and the young. Workers collect nectar and pollen. They produce wax to build cells for honey, pollen, and young bees. Male drones mate once and then die.

⭐ Queen bee.

How are honey bees kept in hives? Carefully. The bees are wild. A hive can hold up to 50,000 bees. It can produce from 50 to 200 pounds of honey in a year.

⭐ A beekeeper extracts honey from honeycombs.

For one pound of honey, bees have to travel a long way. The total distance bees travel to produce a pound of honey equals three trips around the world. Honey and other bee products are believed to have many health benefits.

Honey bees are not native to North America. European settlers brought them in the 1600s. U.S. beekeepers now keep about 2.4 million hives. Most of them are shipped around the country to pollinate crops. More than 1.5 million hives visit almond crops in California each year!

Honey bee boxes line sunflower and lavender fields.

2 What's Happening to Bees?

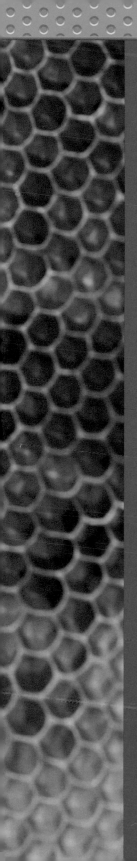

Honey bees are dying in huge numbers all over the world. But they are just the most visible sign of a much bigger problem. Whatever kills honey bees kills other bees, too. Several types of bumblebees are now extinct in Europe. Even more are endangered. The same thing is happening all over the world. In ten years, more than half of the bees in U.S. hives disappeared. Other insect pollinators are also in trouble. Why are they dying? Scientists are trying to find out.

Colony Collapse Disorder (CCD)

In 2006, large numbers of worker bees began to disappear from their hives. The queens and the larvae stayed behind. But no workers took care of them. Colony Collapse Disorder took a massive toll for several years. But we still don't understand it. Scientists now think that the loss is due to a number of factors. Today, about 30% of bee colonies die off. Let's look at some possible causes.

Habitat Loss

Earth's population keeps growing. People need more and more food. So they clear forests—and native plants—to plant crops. Without a variety of pollen, bees are not as healthy.

People plant massive farms with huge swaths of the same plant. The plants on these farms all bloom at once. Nothing blooms between or around them. Bees may no longer have food throughout the growing season. Farmers truck honeybees in to pollinate their plants. The bees shuttle around the country.

★ Forests are being lost world-wide to make space for houses and crops.

People plant lawns that don't flower or feed bees. Great stretches of grass fill yard after yard. Many people plant exotic bushes and flowers that native bees can't use. These plants compete for resources. They crowd out native plants important to bees.

All of this adds up to less food for bees.

With less food, fewer bees survive. They pollinate a smaller number of plants. Fewer plants produce seeds. Fewer new plants grow. Some plants disappear. So do the creatures that feed on them. The problem keeps growing worse.

★ Bees need a variety of flowering plants.

Global Warming

For the past 50 years, the change in Earth's climate has been dramatic. The average global temperature has risen. Faster than ever recorded before.

People are responsible for the change. Burning fossil fuels gives off gases. Carbon dioxide is the main **greenhouse gas**. It traps the sun's heat. That warms the planet.

 Some power plants release carbon dioxide into the atmosphere.

Climate change affects plants. A place where a plant grows can become warmer or cooler. Wetter or drier. Plants disappear from places where they used to grow. They pop up in new areas where the climate did not suit them before.

Climate change can make flowers bloom earlier or later than usual. When bees arrive, the flowers might not yet be open. Or they might have bloomed already. Native bees may not find food. Honey bees are less affected because they can regulate their hive temperature.

Climate change causes extreme weather. Droughts and floods can wipe out bees' food supplies. Severe winters can be stressful for all pollinators. Those that survive might now be weaker.

17

Pesticides: Herbicides and Insecticides

Herbicides are poisons that kill plants. They are used on farms and lawns. They kill many flowering plants that would otherwise feed bees. **Insecticides** are poisons that kill insects. They kill pests in farm fields. They kill bees and other pollinators in yards and parks.

Seeds of some crops are treated with insecticides before they are planted. These chemicals move into pollen and nectar. They damage bees' immune systems. Bees exposed to any insecticides are less able to fight disease. They have trouble collecting pollen.

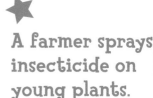 A farmer sprays insecticide on young plants.

Bee Health

Mites and other parasites infect all bee colonies. Viruses spread from bee to bee. Diseases travel around the world, stressing bees and weakening them.

All of these factors combine to make life tougher for bees.

3 What Would We Do Without Bees?

A farmer pollinates apple blossoms by hand.

Could we manage without bees? Not easily. Here are some ways people are trying to cope.

Pollinating by Hand

An area in southwest China has lost most of its native bees. **Pesticides** wiped them out. Since the 1980s, apple farmers there have used an expensive method. Workers climb the trees. They carry paint brushes and pots of pollen. They pollinate apple and pear blossoms by hand. Beekeepers have tried placing beehives in the orchards. But the ongoing poison use kills the bees. Farmers grow fewer apples there now.

Robot Bees

Researchers at Harvard University have created tiny robot bees. These "RoboBees" fly. They can hover and move from side to side. Perhaps they could pollinate crops. They could be useful in small, dangerous places where people could not easily go. Do you think they could ever replace bees?

Our Food Supply

Without bees to pollinate crops, the cost of growing food would rise. Some food plants might disappear. So would the animals that eat them. Food that we eat every day could become too expensive for many people to afford. If fruit and vegetables cost too much, people would eat less healthy foods.

Rice, corn, and wheat are wind pollinated. They release large amounts of pollen into the air. Beans and some other plants pollinate themselves. But beans and grains are not enough. How will Earth support its growing human population?

Research

What do bees need to survive and thrive? We know a great deal about honey bees. But not as much research has focused on other bees. We need to know more about all pollinators.

Birds that eat insects are also disappearing. Is there a link? Scientists are trying to find out. They are studying the effects of pesticides on birds and animals.

★ Birds, like robins, eat harmful insects in lawns and fields.

★ Bees that nest in the ground are affected by tilling and irrigation on farms.

Farming Practices

Studies show that more bees visit farms where wildflowers grow around crop fields. Even small strips of flowers attract bees. Trees and shrubs help boost pollinator numbers, too.

Some farm fields are flooded to irrigate crops. This method can be less expensive than investing in spraying equipment. But it can drown native bees that nest in the ground. Spraying water on crops is safer for bees.

Integrated Pest Management (IPM)

With IPM, farmers try to control pests. At the same time, they try to keep risks to people as low as possible. They try to protect the environment. They identify pests. Farmers work to prevent problems. They monitor their crops. They use natural enemies and other controls. They use pesticides only when needed and in the safest ways possible.

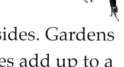

Bee-Friendly Habitats

In some states, flowers bloom along roadsides. Gardens grow around power lines. Many small spaces add up to a big difference.

Pesticide Use

Insects belong in our world. They fit into ecosystems. They function as helpers. They add beauty and wonder. Yet some people grab a can of poison spray whenever they spy an insect. They don't realize that the pesticide kills all insects. Butterflies. Ladybugs. Bees.

The U. S. Environmental Protection Agency (EPA) is trying to help. It is creating labels with clearer warnings. The labels could help protect bees.

Pesticide Bans

The European Union is taking a stand. It banned the use of three **neonicotinoids**. It based the decision on a study that pointed out risks to bees. The ban will last for two years. During that time, new data will be studied. But some farmers are using older pesticides instead. They might be worse for bees, and for people.

Several U.S. cities have passed similar bans. The EPA is re-evaluating these chemicals. First, it must complete new bee safety research. That could take years. In the meantime, bees are still in danger.

Protesters trying to eliminate pesticides.

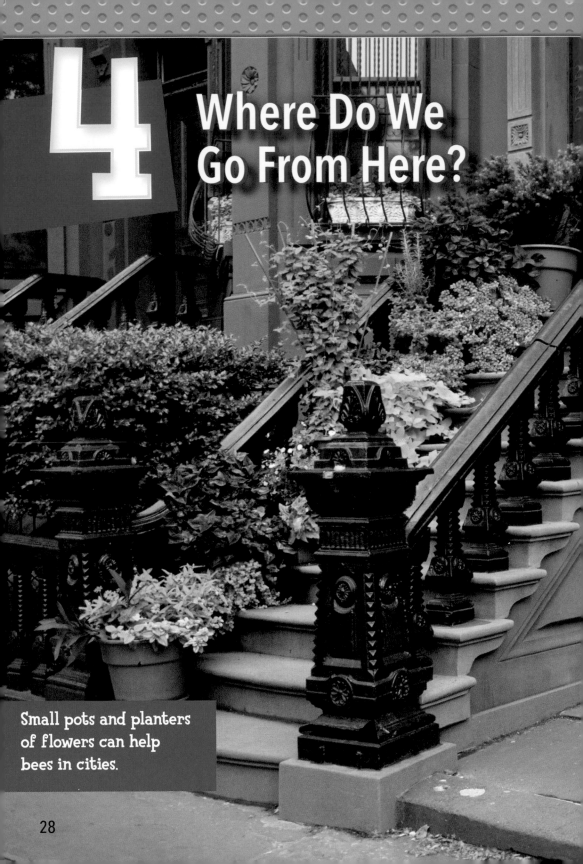

4 Where Do We Go From Here?

Small pots and planters of flowers can help bees in cities.

We all can take action to help protect bees. Here are some ways to help.

Plant a Pollinator Garden

Flower beds are not only prettier than lawns. They also provide food and shelter for bees and other pollinators. Choose native plants that belong in your region. They grow with the area's natural resources. With a variety of flowers, something blooms from spring through fall. Where native plants grow, butterflies appear. So do birds. Fruit and vegetable plants also attract bees. Crops benefit from bee pollination. Even a small city garden can make a difference.

Bees also need fresh water. A dripping faucet can provide a good supply. Flowing water keeps mosquitoes from laying eggs. In a pond, floating plants give bees a place to land so they don't fall in and drown. In a birdbath, stones or corks make good perches. Mud is also useful for some bees.

⭐ This nesting box was built to attract bees and other helpful insects.

Give Bees a Home

Many bees live in holes in the ground. Gardeners can leave some spaces bare to allow them access. A patch of rough grass can provide a bee home. Some bees nest in hollow tubes like plant stems. Pieces of bamboo work well. One end should be open, and one should be closed. A messy pile of old wood and dead branches can host bees and many other creatures. You can also build or buy a bee house.

Limit Pesticide Use

Look for non-chemical solutions for problems with pests. Remove pests by hand if you can. If you must use pesticides, be sure to read the labels. Follow directions carefully. Make sure to protect yourself, too!

Work for Earth

Do what you can to combat global warming. Reduce your energy use. Reuse and recycle. Walk or ride a bike where you can. Carpool. Use public transportation. Encourage voters to vote for Earth-friendly candidates.

Organic fruits and vegetables are grown with only organic pesticides.

Pollinator Health Task Force

In 2014 President Obama created a task force to help pollinators. It focused on honey bees and native bees. It also had to do with the health of birds, bats, and butterflies. The task force included members of many government agencies. It came up with an action plan[1].

The plan has three main goals:

- to reduce honey bee deaths by 50% within 10 years
- to increase the number of Monarch butterflies in 5 years
- to improve 7 million acres of land for pollinators over the next 5 years

The plan includes more research. It should help to make more people aware of bees' plight.

Monarch butterfly populations have also decreased due to herbicide use.

[1] Report released May 2015

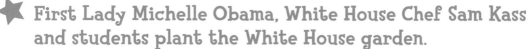
First Lady Michelle Obama, White House Chef Sam Kass and students plant the White House garden.

Bees at the White House

First Lady Michelle Obama tried something new at the White House in 2014. She planted a Pollinator Garden. Students helped her put in the plants. The garden is meant to attract bees and Monarch butterflies. It includes a beehive. People on tours see the hive when they visit. The garden reminds people of the value of pollinators.

What would we do without bees?

Beekeepers report that the cost of maintaining their hives keeps rising. Part of the expense stems from replacing lost bees. Part comes from treating sick bees. At the same time, honey production per hive has dropped to record low levels. Some beekeepers are giving up.

Native bees don't get as much attention as honey bees. But we know that they suffer from the same problems.

Without bees, we would have fewer types of plants. Our world would be less colorful. We would have fewer food choices. We need bees. And bees need our help.

 Smoke calms the bees so the beekeeper can work.

Work for Pollinators

Learn all you can about bees, butterflies, and other pollinators. The more you know, the more you'll appreciate all they do for us! They will continue to help provide our food if we keep them safe.

Volunteer with a pollinator-friendly organization or garden group. Spend time outdoors and enjoy nature. Watch pollinators at work. Then help spread the word!

STEM Career Connections

All over the world, workers are needed in four key areas:

- Science
- Technology
- Engineering
- Math

Scientists work in research labs. They also go out in the world to observe. They collect data to study.

Technology puts science to practical use. Many STEM jobs are related to computers.

Engineers solve problems. They invent and design new products.

Math is a key skill in many kinds of jobs.

Bees need advocates around the world. They'll use math to analyze data. They'll study bees in hives and in their natural habitats. Think up new theories. Explore safer methods. Document changes. They might focus on these and other issues:

- Colony Collapse Disorder and its causes

- safer alternatives to pesticides

- safe, efficient food production

STEM skills help people working with bees and their survival in these fields.

- beekeeping

- education

- farming

- gardening

- landscaping

- pest control

- research

How will bees fit into your future?

Resources

Books

The Buzz on Bees: Why Are They Disappearing?
by Shelley Rotner. Holiday House (2010)

The Case of the Vanishing Honeybees:
A Scientific Mystery by Sandra Markle.
Lerner Publishing Group (2013)

The Hive Detectives: Chronicle of a Honey Bee Catastrophe
by Loree Griffin Burns. HMH Books for Young Readers (2013)

What is Pollination? (Big Science Ideas) by Bobbie Kalman.
Crabtree Publishing (2010)

What if There Were No Bees?: A book about the Grassland Ecosystem
by Suzanne Slade. Picture Window Books (2010)

Web Sites and Videos

Bee: http://kids.sandiegozoo.org/animals/insects/bee

Bees: A Honey of an Idea: http://bees.techno-science.ca/english/bees/

Honeybee: http://www.gpnc.org/honeybee.htm

Plant a Pollinator Garden at Home or School:
http://www.nps.gov/experiences/pollinatorgarden.htm

Plant Parts – Flowers:
http://urbanext.illinois.edu/gpe/case1/c1facts2d.html

Glossary

anther: the part of a plant that produces and holds pollen. It is part of the stamen and is usually held on a stalk called a filament.

colony: a group of plants or animals that live and/or grow together

greenhouse gas: a gas that traps and holds heat in the atmosphere. The main greenhouse gases are carbon dioxide, methane, nitrous oxide, and fluorinated gases.

herbicide: a pesticide that kills plants. Herbicides kill many flowering plants that would otherwise feed bees.

insecticide: a pesticide that kills insects

larva: the immature form of an animal that changes its structure as it matures. Bee larvae hatch from eggs and look like worms. They grow, molt, and change into pupae.

nectar: sweet liquid in flowers that bees feed on

neonicotinoids: agricultural insecticides similar to nicotine in tobacco

pesticide: a chemical used to kill pests or keep them away Herbicides and insecticides are types of pesticides. Other pesticide types are meant to kill fungi, algae, rodents, or other unwanted plants or animals.

pollen: the powdery male reproductive cells of a plant, produced in the anthers of flowers

pollinate: to move pollen from the anther of a flower to the stigma, usually on another flower.

pupa: the stage in an insect's life between larva and adult. During the pupa stage, a bee's body changes from the wormlike larva into the adult shape with three body sections.

stigma: the top part in the center of a flower where pollen germinates

Index